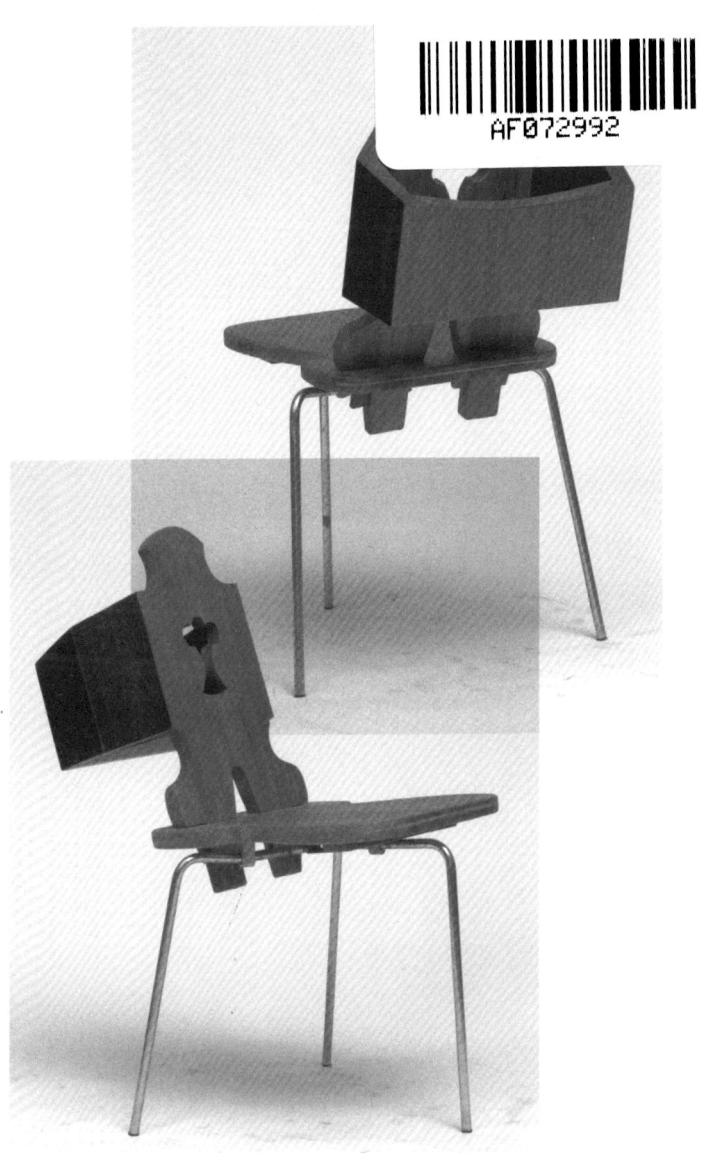

Tirolo (13 DECEMBER 2006) was initially made to hold the leaflets for the *Confronting the Chair* exhibition at the London Design Museum in 2007.

CONTENTS

P. 06	100 Chairs Emily King	P. 33	Deyan Sudjic
P. 14	The Concealing Chair Kate Kilalea	P. 62	*We Love Chairs* Michael Marriott
P. 18	19/9/07 Alex Rich	P. 69	*Making Chairs out of Chairs* Ron Arad

Side Effect chair (24 JULY 2006)

100 Chairs in 100 Days and its 100 Ways
Martino Gamper

Backside (3 SEPTEMBER 2007)

100 Chairs in 100 Days and its 100 Ways
        Martino Gamper
First published in Great Britain in 2007 by Dent—De—Leone,
2nd edition 2010, 3rd edition 2012, 4th edition 2016,
5th edition 2022
www.dentdeleone.com
ISBN 978—1—907908—77—4
Edited and designed by Åbäke
Printed by die Keure
Photography: Andreas Sterzing (p. 51), Martino Gamper
and Edward Horsford (p. 49, 50, 52), Angus Mill and Åbäke
(all other)
Texts, images © the authors. All rights reserved in
accordance with the provisions of the Copyright
Designs and Patents Act, 1988.

                              www.gampermartino.com

Split (25 JULY 2007)

P. 81 The Process of Making One Hundred Chairs
       Martino Gamper

P. 85 1 000 000 Thoughts while Sitting, part III
       Åbäke

P. 93 Martino Gamper is _____
       (an Update from his previous book)
       Kajsa Ståhl

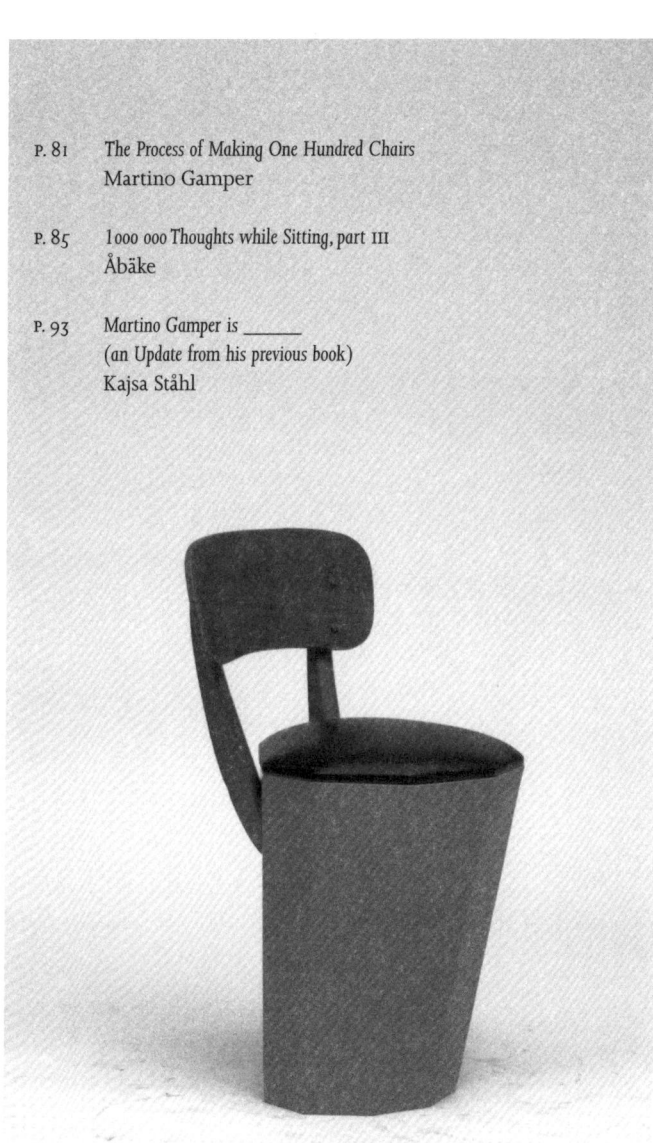

Arnoldone (13 SEPTEMBER 2007)

100 Chairs
Emily King

Martino Gamper's 100 chairs invite organisation. Their quantity and their combination of sameness and difference prompt the curatorial urge to arrange, sort and categorise. But how to go about such a task? Gamper himself offers few clues. He has recorded the day each chair was made, but chronological arrangement does not seem to be the answer. While later designs do tend toward complexity, and also hint more often at human or animal representation, it is impossible to make out a single, useful developmental strand.

Size OO (18 MAY 2007)

Likewise, he has given the chairs names — *Purple Collar*, for example, for a chair with a shoulder-high wing of coloured plastic or *Olympia* for a seat supported on a network of rings — but again, these terms seem more like mnemonics, devices for bringing the pieces to mind, rather than the keys to their essences. Turning to other schemes, perhaps the chairs could best be sorted according to their constituent parts. Some of them contain elements of well-known pieces by celebrated designers, others are constructed from generic, anonymous seating and a few have parts that come from other fields entirely. This exercise, while initially satisfying (particularly in pandering to the current obsession with authored products),

Rock'n Roll (13 AUGUST 2006)

eventually fails to fix the objects. As vacillating in appearance as Wittgenstein's duckrabbit drawing, it is possible on first glance to see the chairs as assemblies of diverse elements, yet on the second to perceive them as singular pieces. To report on only one of these aspects is not enough.

Moving away from the media-driven, consumer-oriented perspective of designer furniture, would it be appropriate to categorise the chairs in a more production focused fashion according to their materials? A very basic list includes wood, metal, plastic, foam, cloth and tape. Add to that the complexity of techniques, both those of making the original ingredients

Hanger (22 SEPTEMBER 2006)

and that of combining them into a single new chair, and an extremely descriptive, highly detailed system begins to emerge. In its favour, this scheme reflects the spontaneity of method that is at the heart of the 100 chairs project, but to its detriment it would be incredibly complex, just about every chair demanding a category of its own.

Another potential system of organisation is shape: grouping the chairs into the round, the square and the triangular; sorting between the curvaceous and the sharp-edged; distinguishing between the solid and the spindly. Or what about calling in Goldilocks to conduct a comfort test, to judge

Barbapapa in Vienna (07 AUGUST 2006) was made in Vienna using a classic Thonet chair together with a stretchy pipe-dress.

the too hard, the too soft and the just right? Or, on a slightly more technical note, the chairs could be arranged according to their numbers of legs or types of base. Thinking along these lines, there is a good subset of seats that are only stable if sat on at a certain angle, braced in a particular way. Maybe means of balance could become an unorthodox basis for curatorial distinction?

Double Sonnet (05 AUGUST 2006)

All of these systems apply to Gamper's 100 chairs and all are useful in clarifying their nature, but not one of them fully accounts. Given that the designer's method hinges on the highly skilled but essentially ad hoc overthrow of standard production processes, perhaps this challenge to an orderly worldview is only to be expected. Maybe the nature of the 100 chairs will only become clear once they leave studios and galleries behind and spend some time in the world beyond relating to seats of other sorts.

Spring Loaded (22 JULY 2006)

Opposite page: *Plank Rocker* (03 JUNE 2006)

Hands On (27 september 2006)

The Concealing Chair
    Kate Kilalea

It's 2am beneath the hidden moon.
The brown leather armchair is concealing Daniel and a book.
His unwashed hair sticks over the top like a toy
from the toy box but his eyes are soft and sleepy-looking.

The lights are all out but one. If the chair were made of glass
I would've known that he was wearing nothing
but his blue t-shirt and beneath it, blue underpants,
and a pair of skinny-legs like a girl or a deer.

Black Skirt (13 APRIL 2006)

Daniel is the part of the chair which is useless,
the bit sits and reads. His book sails calmly and evenly on his
breathing chest but he grips it with both hands, tightly, like a
photograph or a bank note. My pen is scratching at the
kitchen table and city birds sing anxiously at the window.
It's almost Monday morning but we're not yet sleeping
and we've left the dishes from dinner sitting in the sink,

Side Chair Drawer (27 SEPTEMBER 2006)

not yet clean, and there is a scratching sound
coming from deep down in Daniel's beard
which is dry and so incessantly itchy that I should've
guessed it was hiding something too.

Charles and Ply (28 JULY 2006)

Ghost (12 SEPTEMBER 2007)

19/9/07

    Alex Rich

On 19/9/07, Alex Rich <alex@field-trip.org> wrote:
In a way this text by Richard Serra is a readymade
which relates to Mr. Gamper. The verb list was something
I always liked.

Alex

Lap-dog (27 JULY 2006)

> .
> When I first started, what was very, very important to me was
> dealing with the nature of process. So what I had done is I'd
> written a verb list: to roll, to fold, to cut, to dangle, to twist...
> and I really just worked out pieces in relation to the verb list
> physically in a space. Now, what happens when you do that is
> you don't become involved with the psychology of what you're
> making, nor do you become involved with the after image of
> what it's going to look like.

Front to back (3 AUGUST 2007)

> So, basically it gives you a way of proceeding with material in
> relation > to body movement, in relation to making, that
> divorces from any notion of metaphor, any notion of easy
> imagery.

— Richard Serra,
http://www.pbs.org/art21/artists/serra/clip1.html

Plastic Roland (15 JULY 2006)

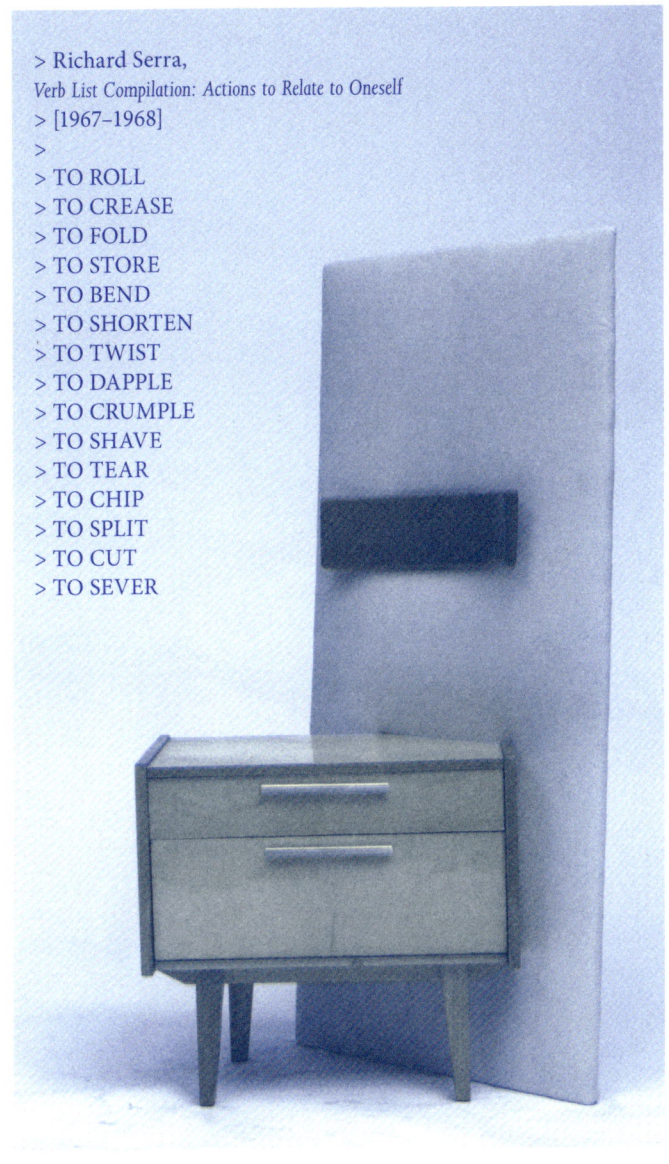

> Richard Serra,
> *Verb List Compilation: Actions to Relate to Oneself*
> [1967–1968]
>
> TO ROLL
> TO CREASE
> TO FOLD
> TO STORE
> TO BEND
> TO SHORTEN
> TO TWIST
> TO DAPPLE
> TO CRUMPLE
> TO SHAVE
> TO TEAR
> TO CHIP
> TO SPLIT
> TO CUT
> TO SEVER

Caritas (2 SEPTEMBER 2006)

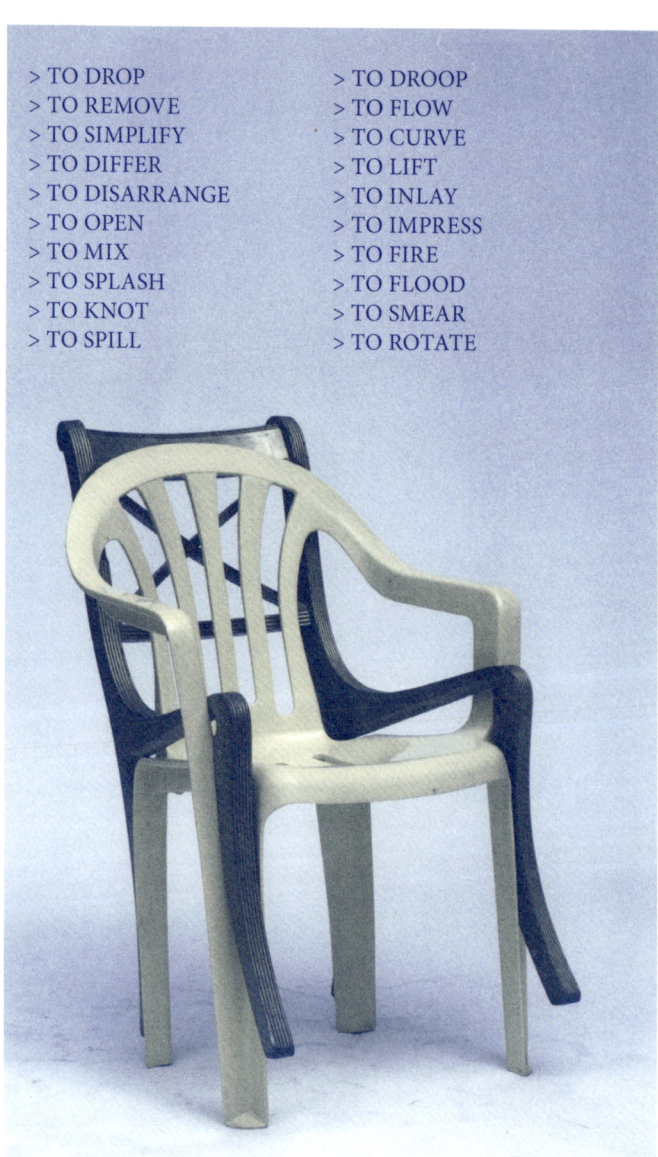

> TO DROP
> TO REMOVE
> TO SIMPLIFY
> TO DIFFER
> TO DISARRANGE
> TO OPEN
> TO MIX
> TO SPLASH
> TO KNOT
> TO SPILL

> TO DROOP
> TO FLOW
> TO CURVE
> TO LIFT
> TO INLAY
> TO IMPRESS
> TO FIRE
> TO FLOOD
> TO SMEAR
> TO ROTATE

Two-some (14 JULY 2006)

> TO SWIRL
> TO SUPPORT
> TO HOOK
> TO SUSPEND
> TO SPREAD
> TO HANG
> TO COLLECT
> OF TENSION
> OF GRAVITY
> OF ENTROPY

> OF NATURE
> OF GROUPING
> OF LAYERING
> OF FELTING
> TO GRASP
> TO TIGHTEN
> TO BUNDLE
> TO HEAP
> TO GATHER
> TO SCATTER

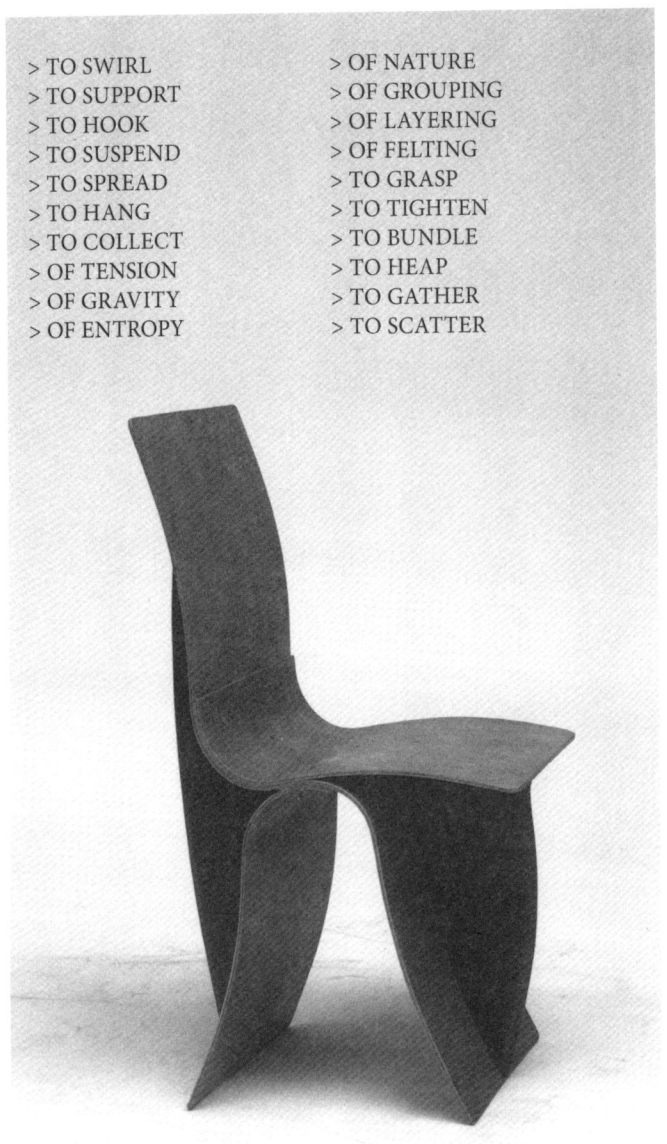

Ply on Ply (20 JULY 2005) uses the plywood seats of old school chairs.

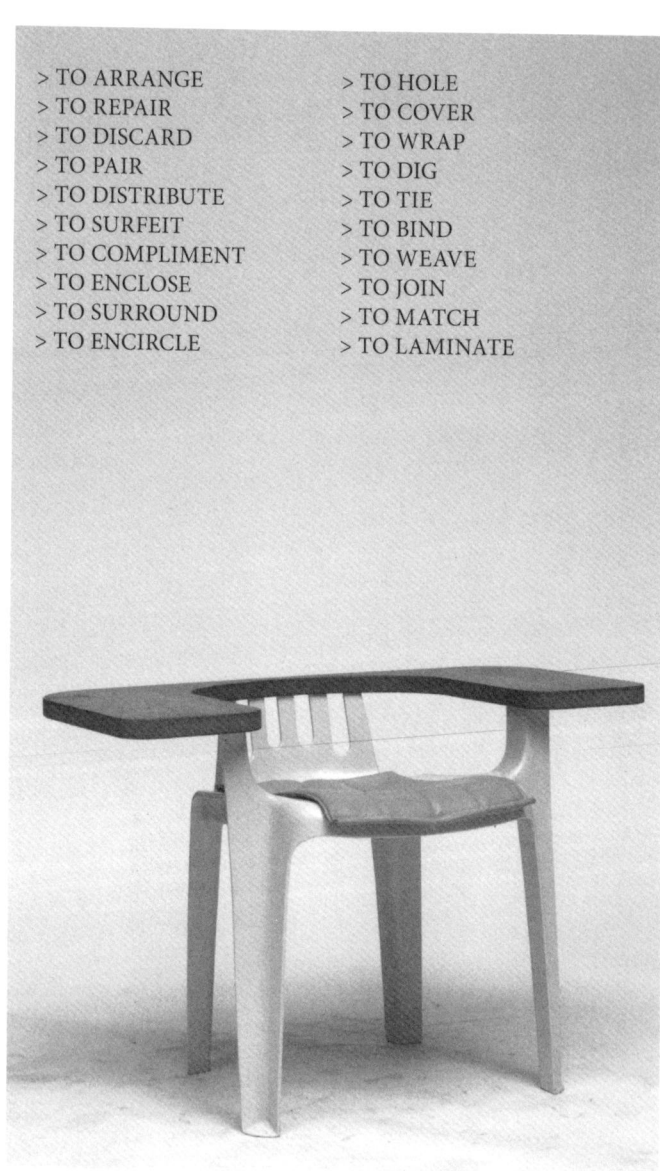

- > TO ARRANGE
- > TO REPAIR
- > TO DISCARD
- > TO PAIR
- > TO DISTRIBUTE
- > TO SURFEIT
- > TO COMPLIMENT
- > TO ENCLOSE
- > TO SURROUND
- > TO ENCIRCLE
- > TO HOLE
- > TO COVER
- > TO WRAP
- > TO DIG
- > TO TIE
- > TO BIND
- > TO WEAVE
- > TO JOIN
- > TO MATCH
- > TO LAMINATE

Cathedra rassa (4 AUGUST 2006)

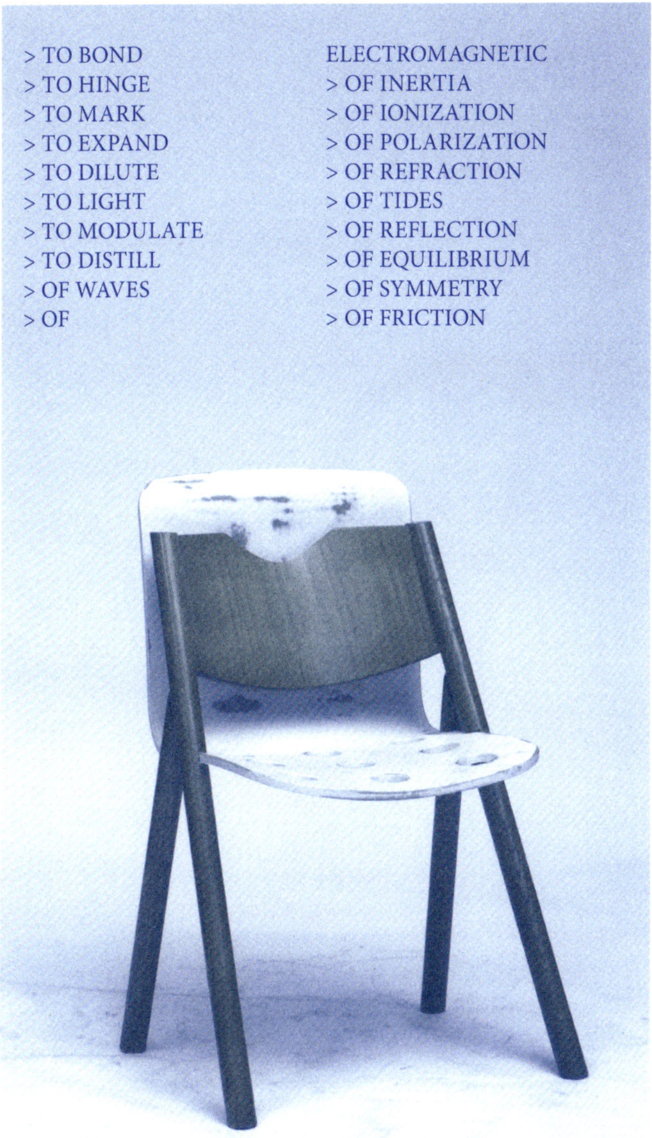

> TO BOND
> TO HINGE
> TO MARK
> TO EXPAND
> TO DILUTE
> TO LIGHT
> TO MODULATE
> TO DISTILL
> OF WAVES
> OF

ELECTROMAGNETIC
> OF INERTIA
> OF IONIZATION
> OF POLARIZATION
> OF REFRACTION
> OF TIDES
> OF REFLECTION
> OF EQUILIBRIUM
> OF SYMMETRY
> OF FRICTION

Jules with Friend (5 AUGUST 2006)

> TO STRETCH
> TO BOUNCE
> TO ERASE
> TO SPRAY
> TO SYSTEMATIZE
> TO REFER
> TO FORCE
> OF MAPPING
> OF LOCATION
> OF CONTEXT
> OF TIME
> OF CABONIZATION
> TO CONTINUE
>
> http://www.ubu.com/concept/serra_verb.html

Claudia and Shona (14 SEPTEMBER 2007)

Chair Bank (12 APRIL 2006)

Rainer Plastic (15 JULY 2006)

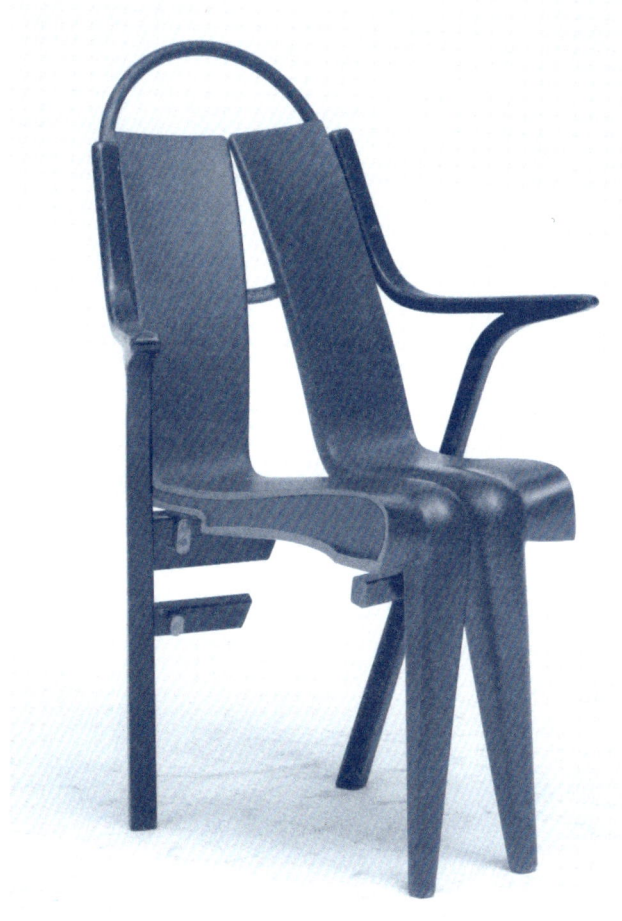

Philippe Fantastique (15 SEPTEMBER 2007)

Plastic-fly (11 SEPTEMBER 2007)

Supporter (14 april 2006)

Achille's Bicicletta (21 SEPTEMBER 2006) is a homage to the greatest Italian designer of the last century Achille Castiglioni.

Deyan Sudjic

The chair has been around long enough to have taken on an authority of its own, distinct from the people who sit in it. The result is a confusion of sign with substance. There are seats of power, country seats, ex cathedra pronouncements, tenured chairs and of course, chairmen, to say nothing of those occupying hot seats, driving seats, back seats and cabinet seats. The chair at heart is an object that must be described as being useful, and yet it is also regarded as culturally significant

because it has such a long history, one that is so closely associated with so many purposes that go far beyond utility.

It's no wonder that the history of modern design is so often told as a sequence of chairs, rather than of cars, or handguns, or typefaces. There are so many extraordinary objects that take the form of chairs, that to see them as a microcosm of the world of design is an entirely plausible idea.

Fixed (14 APRIL 2006)

Chairs certainly take us through a series of key technological episodes in the evolution of design. After endless centuries in which carving, turning and joining wood defined the parameters of chair design, the pace changed dramatically in the 19th century, when the Thonet family transformed furniture into a fully industrial process. Michael Thonet deskilled furniture making by investing in machinery and inventing new techniques that could produce complex shapes without depending on craft skills.

Giro (12 SEPTEMBER 2007) I found the bike frame in Camden on my way to meet Emily.

After bentwood, furniture designers worked with another newly invented material, tubular steel, and then with a huge range of synthetic plastic and glass reinforced fibre, with aluminium casting, and plastic and aluminium extrusions and rotational moulding. In this sense, the chair is a striking reflection of the shifts in technology, production technique and aesthetics. If you were a William Morris, Thonet's patents would have been a development as unwelcome as the McDonald's empire's contribution to world cuisine to anybody with an interest in nutrition. Martino Gamper has put the

Springbock (3 MARCH 2007)

quality of making back into chair design in a radical and unexpected way.

After wood came tubular steel, the emblematic material of the machine age. Marcel Breuer, Mart Stam, and Mies van der Rohe, three of the Modern Movement's key figures, all developed their own versions of the cantilevered chair within months of each other at the start of the 1920s. In chair design terms, it had the impact of electricity on lighting. Tubular steel could be bent into tight, springy curves

Darth Vador (8 SEPTEMBER 2007) is a slight transformation of a go-kart seat into a *Star Wars* character.

supplanting the conventional one leg at each corner format for the chair. There had been technically similar chairs before, devised by anonymous American engineers. But Breuer, Stam and Mies were doing something else. They wanted to use familiar domestic objects to make a point about the modern world. They might not be able to actually build utopia, but Stem could at least pay a plumber to knock up something that hinted at what a utopian machine age might one day look like, with the aid of nothing much more than a few feet of gas pipe. Marcel Breuer made something much more polished for

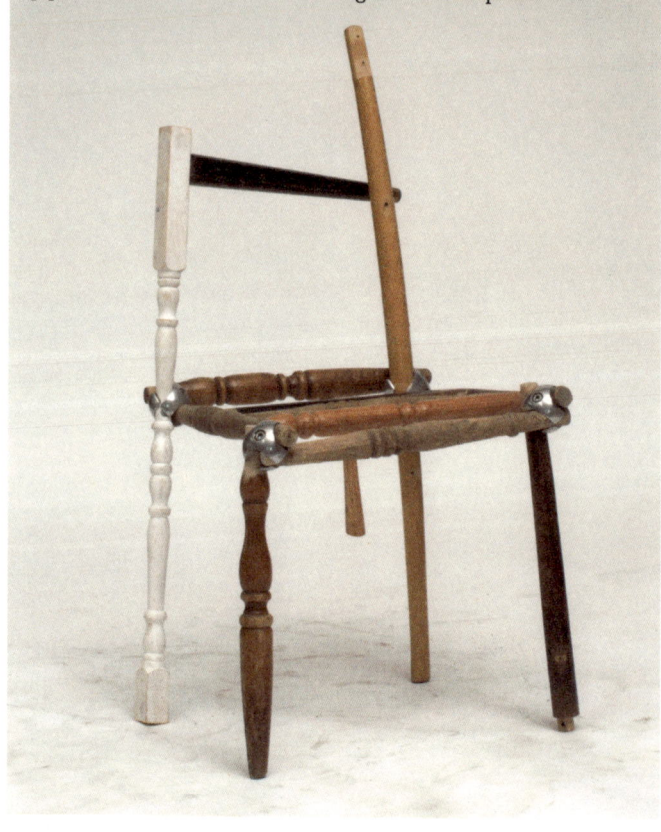

Leg-o (14 SEPTEMBER 2007) After taking apart many of the found chairs I ended up with a lot of single legs.

use at the Bauhaus, while Mies transformed the cantilever into a languid streak of glittering classicism. Eileen Gray celebrated the poetry of mechanisms in her sparely elegant adjustable chairs, lights, tables and mirrors.

A generation later, Charles Eames put the lessons of what in the 1940s was regarded as advanced aircraft manufacturing technology to work, and made chairs out of moulded plywood and fibreglass, shaping profiles of birdlike elegance. Ettore Sottsass was less interested in technique than in form, and

Olympia (2 AUGUST 2006)

pattern, and used the chair as the point of departure for a long drawn out series of speculations on the nature of ritual, and symbol. But these represent only that tiny fraction of chairs whose designers' names we know. There is an astonishingly rich field of the anonymous industrial vernacular that offers even more promising material.

Inflation (16 SEPTEMBER 2006)
Opposite page: *Multiple Choice* (17 SEPTEMBER 2007)

Holding Together (23 MAY 2006)

Juxtaposition (17 DECEMBER 2006) was made as part of a performance — video documentation, shown at the London Design Museum (*Confronting the Chair*, 2007).

Painters Mate (18 MAY 2007)
Thonet meets Jackobsen meets Thonet.

Bare Light (23 SEPTEMBER 2006) Found in Milano, made in Vienna.

oobmaB chair (30 JULY 2006)
Opposite page: *Tubolare* (10 SEPTEMBER 2007)
Rupert always has some chairs waiting to be used.

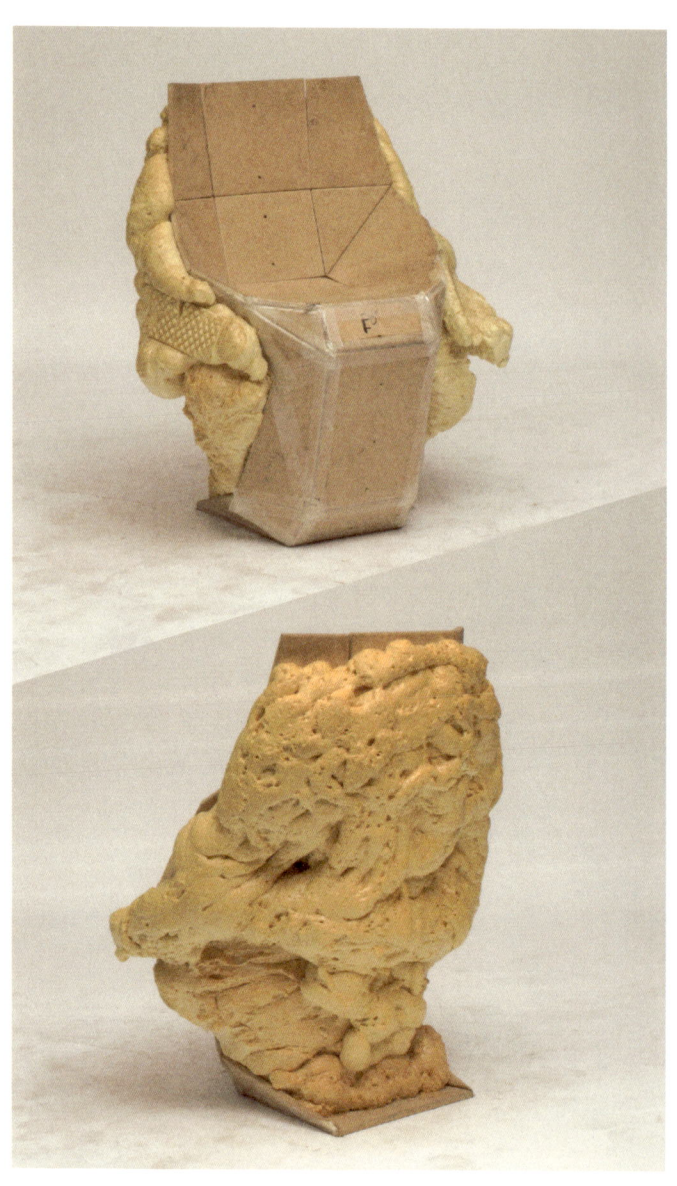

Foam Follows Function (10 OCTOBER 2006)

Kiss Chair (21 JULY 2006)
Gamper was amused by the backrest of the Blue Chair which looks like a pair of lips kissing.

INNESTO, Rubbing up the wrong tree — Martino Gamper

Grafting is used when a gardener wants to grow a new branch onto an established plant. The graft can lead the specimen to generate something very different out of its original form. Hollow tubular parts was the starting point of this project. Printed on the occasion of Martino Gamper's solo show INNESTO, Rubbing up the wrong tree at Nilufar Depot, Milano, June 2022.

ISBN: 978—1—907908—75—0

For more books from Dent—de—Leone please visit www.dentdeleone.com

Back Seat (23 JULY 2006)

Purple Collar (12 april 2006)
Sonnet Butterfly (16 august 2006)

The Arnold Circus Stool — Martino Gamper

The story of a stool, from its origin as a necessary furniture to repopulate a disused park in East London to becoming an ubiquitous sight in international art centres and people's homes in New Zealand or South Korea. Martino Gamper's Arnold Circus Stool accompanies its creator and the friends around him on a nearly 2 decades of local going global in colourful fashion.

ISBN: 978—1—907908—65—1

Ch'*Air N° 9 Chair* (19 JULY 2006)
A chair that joins Jasper Morrison's Air Chair with a bentwood Thonet chair N° 9.

Column (5 august 2007)

Brick-Lane Beauty (first made in 2005 modified on 18 SEPTEMBER 2007)
Chair found and fabric bought a stone's throw from each other.

Breathing Chair (25 september 2006)

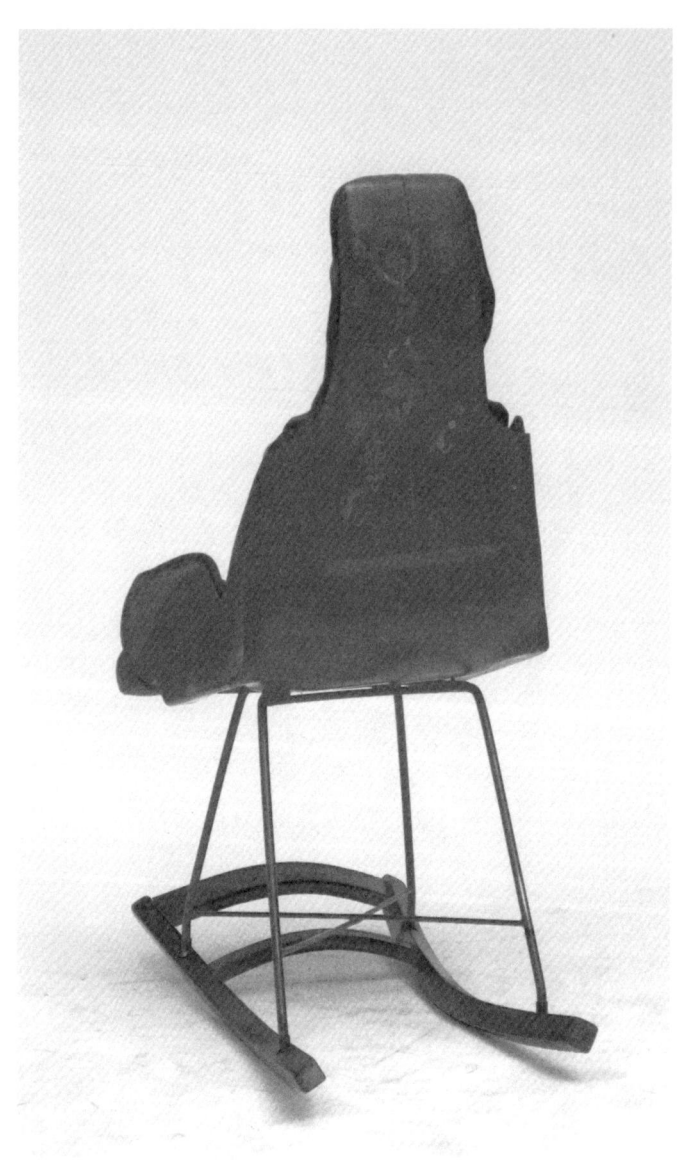

Race against the Chair (4 SEPTEMBER 2007)

Alpino (7 JULY 2006)

Un-stable (2 SEPTEMBER 2007)

Vespino (23 september 2007)
This is what we called a "Yankee" seat (when I got my first Vespa), it was the coolest thing one could put on a Vespa, it was about having a special elevated seat for the person seating on the back (the girl one always fancied).

Plastic on Wood (3 SEPTEMBER 2007)

Arnoldino (10 AUGUST 2006) *The stool designed for Arnold Circus in east London is used for various community events. This is a slightly more comfortable evolution.*

We Love Chairs
    Michael Marriott

We love chairs: old chairs, new chairs, wooden chairs,
metal chairs, plastic chairs, upholstered chairs, broken chairs,
fixed chairs, painted chairs, anonymous chairs, designer
chairs, folding chairs, café chairs, side chairs, arm chairs,
stacking chairs, linking chairs, auditorium chairs, swivel
chairs, moulded chairs, recycled chairs, green chairs, red
chairs, leather chairs, kitchen chairs, dining chairs, office
chairs, school chairs, children's chairs, hairdresser's chairs,
deck chairs, inflatable chairs, garden chairs, high chairs, low
chairs, comfy chairs, beautiful chairs, ugly chairs, three-legged
chairs, kit chairs, lightweight chairs, heavy chairs, shiny

Danish (22 SEPTEMBER 2007)

chairs, wheelchairs, musical chairs, electric chairs, bentwood chairs, plywood chairs, fibreglass chairs, home-made chairs, mass produced chairs, Italian chairs, Egyptian chairs, antique chairs, modern chairs, postmodern chairs, soft chairs, hard chairs, reclining chairs, high-tech chairs, low-tech chairs, cheap chairs, expensive chairs, cantilever chairs, monocoque chairs, library chairs, cane chairs, iconic chairs, odd chairs, stolen chairs, found chairs, other people chairs, Rietveld's chair and Martino's chairs.

Bamboo (30 JULY 2006)

Mono Suede (3 MARCH 2005) was the first chair made in
the series of the hundred chairs, somehow still my favourite one.

Handling (5 SEPTEMBER 2007)

Musical Chair (15 MAY 2006)

Barbamamma (8 august 2006)

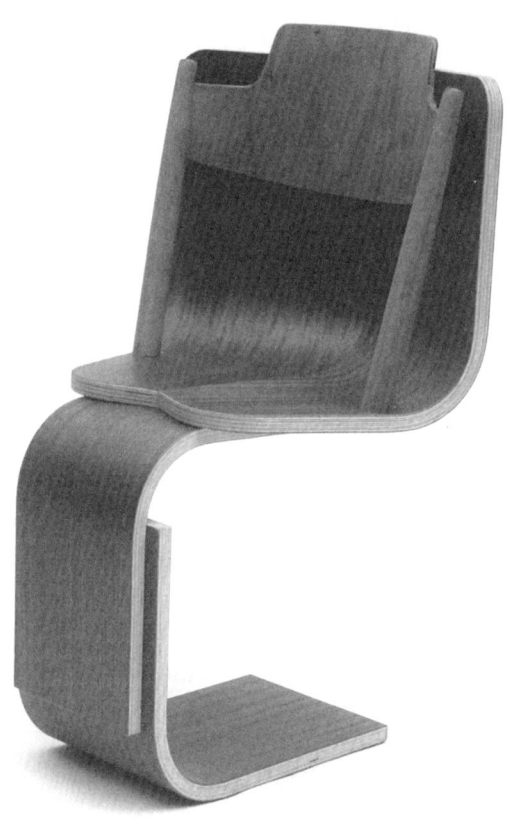

Another Chair in Plywood (10 MARCH 2006)

Making Chairs out of Chairs
    Ron Arad

I met Martino when he was a young student in Vienna, he was not in my class then, I think he was the only boy amongst the girls in the ceramic class. My students worked on "design a step ladder" project. Martino gatecrashed the project and turned up in the exhibition with his contribution; a tall A-frame wooden ladder on the top of which he attached a leather horse saddle. It seems that Martino's passion for making things out of things that are already things started very early, maybe it was always there. Recently, one Sunday night Martino came to our house to collect some ageing

Aradson (21 SEPTEMBER 2007)

(gracefully) Arne Jacobsen chairs and a cracked (no grace) F.P.E of mine. On Monday morning I found in my e-mail a delightful image of a brand new red Martino Gamper chair. Although it was made entirely out of 2 Jacobsen's, it was a total Gamper; clever, poetic, gentle. It made me pleasantly anxious to imagine what life might my dead F.P.E is going to be graced with. You might think that Martino is like some wizard, inventive chef… But then, Martino is a wizard, inventive chef, another passion of his we are lucky to enjoy.

Arne Cubista (9 SEPTEMBER 2007)

Replica (15 JUNE 2007)

Cubo (13 MARCH 2006)

Mono-Jackobsen 2 (1 APRIL 2005)

Copy and Paste (5 MARCH 2006)
Opposite page: *Hollow* (20 SEPTEMBER 2007)

Black and Silver (29 JULY 2006)

Vicky (17 SEPTEMBER 2006) The base was found in Hackney Wick and its backrest in Victoria Park; they were meant to meet each other.

Gymnastic (16 SEPTEMBER 2006)

Turn over (16 SEPTEMBER 2007)

The Process of Making One Hundred Chairs
    Martino Gamper

I didn't make one hundred chairs just for myself or even in an effort to rescue a few hundred unwanted chairs from the streets. The motivation was the methodology: the process of making, of producing and absolutely not striving for the perfect one.

This kind of making was very much about restrictions rather than freedom. The restrictions were key: the material, the style or the design of the found chairs and the time available

Ruberto (10 SEPTEMBER 2007)

— just a 100 days. Each new chair had to be unique, that's what kept me working toward the elusive one-hundredth chair.

I collected discarded chairs from London streets (or more frequently, friends' homes) over a period of about two years. My intention was to investigate the potential of creating useful new chairs by blending together the stylistic and structural elements of the found ones. The process produced something like a three-dimensional sketchbook, a collection of possibilities. I wanted to question the idea of there being an

Paste and Copy (6 MARCH 2006)

innate superiority in the one-off and used this hybrid technique to demonstrate the difficulty of any one design being objectively judged THE BEST.

I also hope my chairs illustrate — and celebrate — the geographical, historical and human resonance of design: what can they tell us about their place of origin or their previous sociological context and even their previous owners? For me, the stories behind the chairs are as important as their style or even their function.

Cornutto (24 SEPTEMBER 2007)

I wanted the project to stimulate a new form of design-thinking and to provoke debate about the value, functionality and the appropriateness of style for certain types of chair. What happens to the status and potential of a plastic garden chair when it is upholstered with luxurious yellow suede? The approach is elastic, highlighting the importance of contextual origin and enabling the creative potential of random individual elements spontaneously thrown together.

The process of personal action that leads towards making rather than hesitating.

Rocker (7 AUGUST 2007)

1000 000 Thoughts while Sitting, part III
    Åbäke

23)
Not many animals walk on two legs. Most of the birds, some monkeys and us. Even fewer sit on anything other than what nature provides: the ground, a branch, a rock. While animals go to where the seats are, we make them; light enough to move around a big table in the living room or to place next to the fishing lake.

24)
At college, we made fun of furniture designers by calling them "chair designers". Beyond juvenile arrogance, I guess we only wondered why people would still want to make new chairs; something so essentially trivial and ubiquitous. Surely someone had already come up with the perfect chair?

Armlength (28 august 2007)

25)
Chairs are signifiers. In the end of *Back to the Future* (Robert Zemeckis, 1985) the main character Marty McFly has come back from the past where he changed his parents for the better. Instead of a bullied loser, his father is now a successful writer and a confident husband. How do we know this? Because of the *Wassily* chairs (Marcel Breuer, 1925) in their living room. The logic is: if they can afford Breuer's classics, they surely are people of taste.

26)
Ten years later, Marcel's creation plays a role in another movie, *The Edukators* (Hans Weingartner, 2004). Peter and Jan are liberal activists who break into luxurious villas but don't steal

Velvet Underneath (16 AUGUST 2006)

anything. Instead, they rearrange furniture and leave a note to the owners: YOUR DAYS OF PLENTY ARE OVER. The *Cheska* chairs (Marcel Breuer, 1928) are made into a tower of the luxury they have somehow become to represent.

27)
Looking at old interior magazines is fun. Look how they decorated in the 70s, 80s or the 90s. Now, what's funny is the presence then and today of the Mies, the Corbus or other modernist classics as the constant feature.

A Basketful (18 AUGUST 2006)

28)
In *Dawn of the Dead* (George Romero, 1978) there's no more room in hell. As a consequence the dead walk the earth. A few survivors take refuge in a shopping mall and desperately try to live on. Their new habitat is rough and cardboard boxes are used as tables. The end of the world is nigh and there is no time for superfluous luxury. However, if you shift your attention from the action to what main man Peter is sitting on, it presents an impossibility which remains a mystery to this day: a cardboard Zig-zag chair (Gerrit Rietveld, 1932–34). Will modernism survive the Apocalypse?

Mono-Jackobsen 1 (12 MARCH 2005)

29)
We've never seen Martino's chairs in a movie but if they were to star, they'd share the screen with a lot of food as well as a lot of people eating it, whilst no doubt discussing equally insignificant and quintessential subject matters.

30)
Kenneth Ståhl told us about the inspiration for *Plankan* (Börge Lindau & Bo Lindekrantz, 1985). A man on a beach stuck a plank of wood in the sand and used his towel to rest his head. For a little while we wondered how such a simple anecdote had turned into a rather complicated chair. Then again not everybody has a beach.

Plastic Fantastic (19 JULY 2006)

Monkey vs Bull (2 AUGUST 2007) A small children's chair that transforms from a Monkey into a Bull.

31)
36 N°14 Thonet chairs (Michael Thonet, 1859) fit in one cubic meter. Better than 36 people fitting in a Mini.

Sonnet Butterfly (16 AUGUST 2006) See also p. 51

Mikado (4 March 2007)
Opposite page: Ferrarista (18 september 2007)

Martino Gamper is _____ (an Update from his previous book)
(edition 5 comments)
  Kajsa Ståhl

Martino Gamper
is a chef; (loves adding ginger, doesn't eat breakfast)
is a furniture designer; (and more)
sold his Volvo for another one (Silver); (doesn't own a car anymore)
likes leather; (but looking for alternatives)
has about twenty chairs around his kitchen table;
misses half of all airplanes he bought tickets for; (less flights)
gives his mobile phone number to his students at the RCA;
      (stopped teaching)

always misses the deadlines but still manages to finish
         the job; (is now on time, with thanks to Francis)
owes Harry a thank you; (still)
cooks for his interns; (cooks for his staff)
likes FileMaker™ Pro;
drives everywhere; (walks everywhere)
sometimes has a moustache;
loves his Bimbi food processor; (new generation available)
has a mum who cooks the best tomato pasta; (family is all)
carries his keys around his neck;
finds good new use of old material;
takes chances;
is a last minute perfectionist;
chews ginger;

A Small Children's Chair that Looks like an Animal or a Scooter
(2 AUGUST 2007)

has designed beermats; (prefers kombucha now)
has made 100 chairs in three years; (and so many more now)
says yes; (working on the NO alternative)
takes the plane to Italy to go for a walk in the mountains;
       (now lives in England, Italy & almost New Zealand,
       so much less flying as longer stays)
doesn't watch TV;
invents theories (ask about the pyramid one)
                          (or the circle one).

Red on Red (17 SEPTEMBER 2007)

Acknowledgements

Firstly and most importantly I would like to thank Harry Thaler and all my interns who helped me on this project over almost 3 years. Their engagement and belief were key in making this project happen.

Omback (31 AUGUST 2006)

Special thanks to: Åbäke, Adam Kershaw, Adam & Maria, Alex Rich, Anna Stewart, Aram Gallery, Clive & Anthony, Corinne Quinn, Da Sul Kim, David & Janice Blackburn, Deyan Sudjic, Edward Horsford, Francis Upritchard, Gemma Holt, Hiroko Shiratori, Isabella MacPherson, Ismaël Abdallah, Kate Kilalea, Kirsteen Mackay, Lars Frideen, Leila Macalister,

Rosso Nero (5 JANUARY 2006)

Michael Marriot, Nadine Jarvis, Neville Sykes, Nilufar Gallery, Nina Yashar, Peter Marigold, Rainer Spehl, Ron Arad, Tiina Hakala, Toby Anstruther, Walter Thaler and Jane Withers & a big THANK YOU to all the people who generously donated and found chairs for the project, especially Allison, Alex, Andrew + Andreas, Benjamin, Brit, Broadway market ladies, Corinne, Daniel, Max, Robert, David & Bettina, Francis, Gregor & Anita, Hiroko, Kajsa, Karl Emilio & Fidel, Karl, Leila, Luke, Luke & Tom, Maki, Michael, Neville, Patrick, Rainer, Ron, Rupert, Shona, Walter and Eddie Mundy. THANK YOU also to Benaki Museum, City Gallery Wellington, MIMOCA, The NRW-Forum, RMIT Design Hub, Site Le Corbusier de Firminy, South Kensington Estates, Triennale Design Museum, YBCA.

Contrasting (18 MARCH 2006)

Martino Gamper's Dorian Gray

Drawers (19 SEPTEMBER 2007)

The Flying Chair (25 SEPTEMBER 2007)	100 Chairs in 100 Days 5, Cromwell Place, London, UK 2 – 15 OCT 2007
USO (10 MAY 2009) Unidentified Seating Object	UFO The NRW-Forum Dusseldorf, Germany 23 MAY – 05 JUL 2009
Franzele (14 MAY 2009)	Stanze e Camere + 100 Chairs in 100 Days Triennale Design Museum, Milano, Italy 6 OCT – 8 NOV 2009
Golden Gate (7 JULY 2010)	Techno CRAFT Yerba Buena Center for the Arts, San Francisco, USA 10 JUL – 10 OCT 2010
Linzer Schnitte (23 NOVEMBER 2011)	100 Chairs en 100 Jours Eglise Saint-Pierre, Site Le Corbusier de Firminy, France 24 NOV – 27 FEB 2011
Niketino (4 JUNE 2013)	100 Chairs in 100 Days Benaki Museum Athens, Greece 06 JUN – 28 JUL 2013
Circle and Turtle (10 JUNE 2015)	100 Chairs in 100 Days Marugame Genichiro-Inokuma Museum of Contemporary Art, Marugame, Japan 13 JUN – 23 SEP 2015
Springmate (12 FEBRUARY 2016)	100 Chairs in 100 Days RMIT Design Hub Melbourne, Australia 26 FEB – 9 APR 2016
Kiwino (2 APRIL 2017)	100 Chairs in 100 Days City Gallery Wellington, Wellington, New Zealand 8 APR – 9 JULY 2017

The one-hundredth chair changes with each exhibition, as a new one is built for each new venue. Let us know if you are interested in hosting the chair.